Love to Dance

Tap

Angela Royston

Raintree is an imprint of Capstone Global Library
Limited, a company incorporated in England and Wales
having its registered office at 7 Pilgrim Street, London,
EC4V 6LB – Registered company number: 6695582

To contact Raintree:
Phone: 0845 6044371
Fax: + 44 (0) 1865 312263
Email: myorders@raintreepublishers.co.uk
Outside the UK please telephone +44 1865 312262.

Text © Capstone Global Library Limited 2013
First published in hardback in 2013
The moral rights of the proprietor have been asserted.

Edited by Nancy Dickmann, Catherine Veitch,
and Abby Colich
Designed by Cynthia Della-Rovere
Picture research by Elizabeth Alexander
Production by Alison Parsons
Originated by Capstone Global Library Ltd
Printed and bound in China by CTPS

ISBN 978 1 406 24949 1
16 15 14 13 12
10 9 8 7 6 5 4 3 2 1

British Library Cataloguing in Publication Data
Royston, Angela,
Tap. -- (Love to dance)
792.7'8-dc23
A full catalogue record for this book is available from
the British Library.

Acknowledgements
We would like to thank the following for permission
to reproduce photographs: Alamy pp. 14 (© The
Commercial Appeal/ZUMA Wire Service), 18 (©
Photos 12), 24 (© Corbis Premium RF), 27 (© Neil
Setchfield), 28 (© ZUMA Wire Service); Getty Images
pp. 4 (Rob Elliott/AFP), 12 (John Kobal Foundation/
Moviepix), 13 (Michael Ochs Archives), 15 (Mike
Clarke/AFP), 17 (Ethan Miller), 19 (Chris Nash/
Digital Vision), 20 (Donna Ward); Press Association p.
11 (AP Photo/ Danny Johnston); Rex Features pp. 21
(c.Warner Br/Everett), 26 (Steven Peskett); Shutterstock
title page (© AlenKadr), 6 (© Hasan Shaheed), 7 (©
Hannamariah), 8 (© AlenKadr), 10 (© Sean Nel), 16
(© Sean Nel), 25 (© Sean Nel), 29 (© Losevsky Pavel);
TopFoto pp. 5 (ArenaPAL/ Clive Barda), 9 (PERSSON
Johan/ ArenaPAL), 22 (ArenaPAL/Francis Loney);
Woolfson & Tay p. 23 (Shim Sham Tap Jam).

Design features reproduced with permission of
Shutterstock (© Steve Wood, © L.Watcharapol).

Cover photograph of Tap Dogs performing at the
Novello Theatre, London reproduced with permission
Rex Features (Alastair Muir).

We would like to thank Annie Beserra for her invaluable
help in the preparation of this book.

Contents

Some words are shown in bold, **like this**. You can find out what they mean by looking in the glossary.

This is tap dancing!

Tap dancing is loud and energetic. It is amazing how fast tap dancers move their feet to the **rhythm** of the music. Sometimes the only music is the sound of tapping feet.

Why I dance

Champion tap dancer Justin Jackson says: "I'm really into tap dancing. The style that I do allows you to express yourself."

How tap began

Tap became popular in the southern states of America, when the dances and drum music of African Americans became mixed with Irish **step dances** and **clog** dances.

Step dances

Irish dancers wear jig shoes for step dancing. These hard jig shoes are perfect for **striking** the ground.

What to wear

Tap dancers wear special tap shoes. The shoes have metal plates screwed to the **soles** of the toes and the heels. It is the metal plates that make the tapping sound when they hit the floor.

Be comfortable

Some tap dancers dress up in fancy costumes when they perform on stage. But you can tap dance in any comfortable clothes.

Basic step: the shuffle

The shuffle is a basic step. The dancer uses the **ball** of the foot to **brush** the floor going forwards, and **strike** it on the way back.

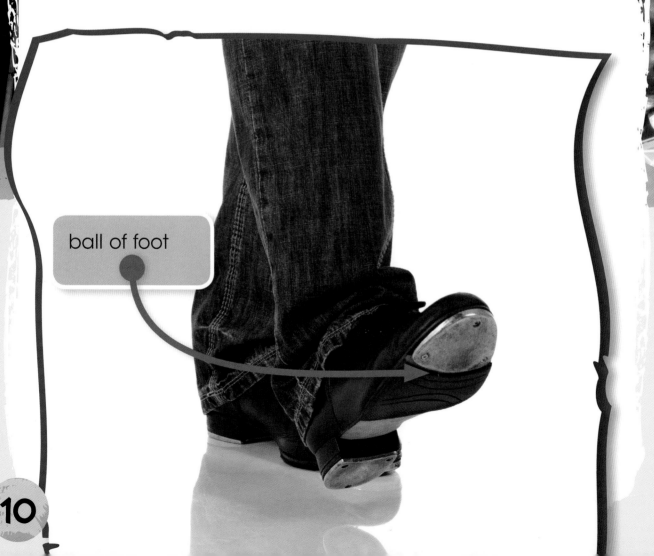

ball of foot

The hop, shuffle, step

In the hop, shuffle, step, the dancer changes from one foot to the other with a hop and a shuffle in between.

The Hollywood years

In the 1930s actors often tap danced in films. In *Singin' in the Rain*, Gene Kelly is so happy, he tap dances in heavy rain! Bill "Bojangles" Robinson was one of the first tap dance film stars.

Fred Astaire and Ginger Rogers were famous for their dance films.

Fast mover

Bojangles claimed he could run backwards faster than most people can run forwards!

Tap dancing skills

Tap dancers have good **rhythm**. They also need good balance and **coordination**, and lots of practice.

14

Record-breaking skill

James Devine is the world's fastest tap dancer. He made 38 taps every second in a dance display in 1998!

15

Tricky move: wings

In a wing, the dancer **brushes** one foot out to the side, **strikes** it on the way back, and then steps on to it. To make it harder, the dancer hops off the ground with the other foot!

brushing a foot

Two feet together

The most spectacular way to do wings is to jump and do the move with both feet at the same time!

Tap dance styles

There are different styles of tap dancing. In **rhythm** tap the dancers learn to **improvise**. This means they make up their own moves as they go along.

Gregory Hines was one of the most famous rhythm tap dancers.

Flamenco

Flamenco is a dance from southern Spain. The dancers tap and stamp their feet and heels. Sometimes they click their fingers, too.

A living legend

Savion Glover is the most amazing tap dancer today. His show *Bring in 'Da Noise, Bring in 'Da Funk* told the history of African Americans through tap dancing.

Savion amazed audiences in his show *Bare Soundz*.

Happy Feet

Happy Feet is a cartoon film about Mumble, a tap dancing penguin. Savion Glover provided the real dancing feet for the cartoon penguin.

The tap dance challenge

Sometimes, dancers face off in a tap dance challenge. One tap dancer begins to dance while the other watches. They take turns in trying to outdo each other's steps and **combinations**.

The Shim Sham Shimmy

The Shim Sham Shimmy is a dance that sometimes all the dancers do together at the end of a performance or festival.

Tricky move: the turn

More skilled tappers put several steps and turns together to make amazing **combinations**. One tricky move is to turn by crossing the feet and swivelling on the toes at the same time.

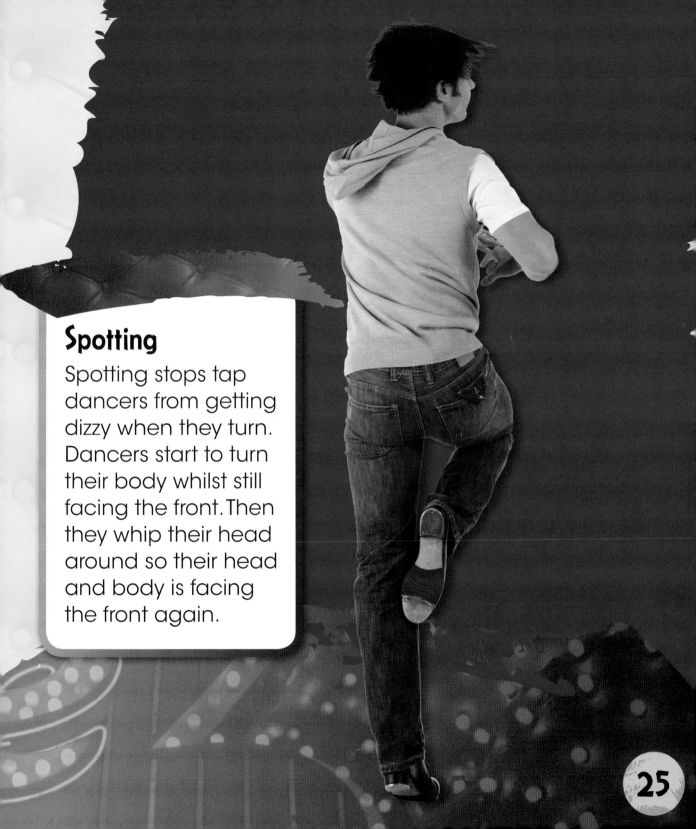

Spotting

Spotting stops tap dancers from getting dizzy when they turn. Dancers start to turn their body whilst still facing the front. Then they whip their head around so their head and body is facing the front again.

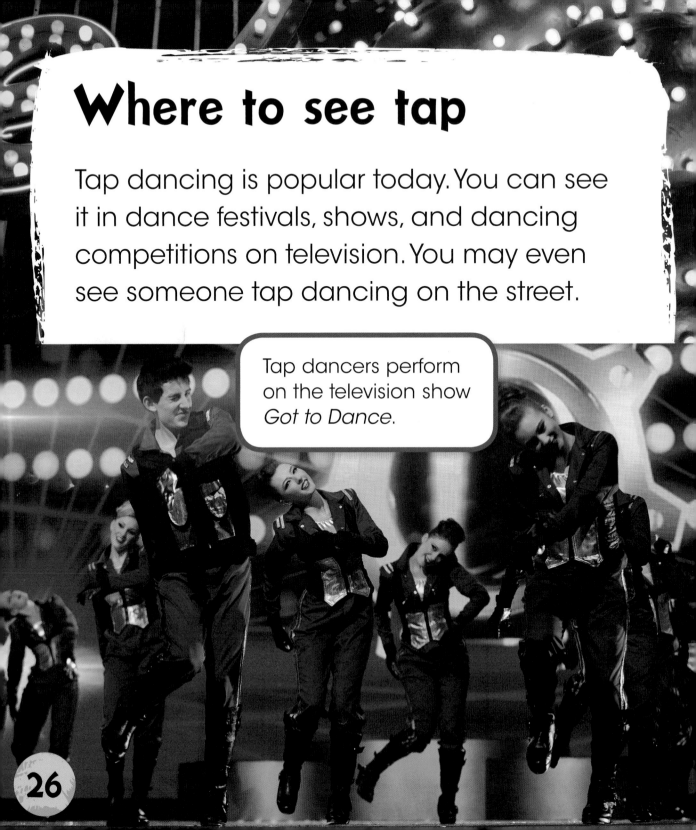

Where to see tap

Tap dancing is popular today. You can see it in dance festivals, shows, and dancing competitions on television. You may even see someone tap dancing on the street.

Tap dancers perform on the television show *Got to Dance.*

These street buskers perform an *a cappella* tap dance.

No music!

A cappella tap dance is a tap dance with no music. The dancers have to keep perfect time by themselves. Some dancers also use their voice to imitate, or copy, the sounds of their feet.

27

Give it a go!

Tap dancing is fun to do and good exercise. You can stamp your feet and make a lot of noise! The best way to learn is to join a tap dance class.

28

New steps

When you learn a new step, do it slowly at first, and then practise until you can do it fast.

Glossary

a cappella without music. *A cappella* tap dance is a tap dance with no music.

ball part of the sole of the foot between the toes and instep

brush in tap dancing, to brush is to bend the knee and strike the ball of the foot across the floor

clog strong, heavy shoe with a wooden sole

combination several steps joined together

coordination move different parts of the body at the same time

improvise make something up as you go along

rhythm regular pattern of sounds linked to the strong beat in a piece of music

sole part of your foot or shoe that touches the ground when you walk

step dance dance in which the movement of the feet is more important than moving the arms or other parts of the body. For example, an Irish step dance.

strike hit

Find out more

Books

Savion Glover, Stephen Feinstein
    (Enslow Elementary, 2008)

Tap and Jazz, Nikki Gamble (Heinemann Library, 2009)

Tap Dancing (Snap Books), Karen M. Graves
    (Capstone Press, 2007)

Tap Dancing, Kathryn Clay (Pebble Plus, 2010)

Websites

www.james-devine.com/media/videos
These two video clips are of James Devine, "the fastest tap dancer on the planet".

www.ehow.com/video_2374557_tap-dancing-kids-part-1.html
This video shows you how to do a simple heel step.

Index